Cathy Glass

The Untold Story of Healing Broken Lives

By

George Aguiar

Copyright © 2024 [George Aguiar]. All rights reserved. This work is protected by copyright law and may not be reproduced, distributed, transmitted, displayed, published, or broadcast without the prior written permission of the copyright owner. You may not alter or remove any trademark, copyright, or other notice from copies of the content. Unauthorized use and/or duplication of this material without express and written permission from the copyright owner is strictly prohibited. Excerpts and links may be used, provided that full and clear credit is given to [George Aguiar] with appropriate and specific direction to the original content.

TABLE OF CONTENTS

Copyright

TABLE OF CONTENTS

INTRODUCTION

CHAPTER ONE

   Early Life and Background

CHAPTER TWO

   The Beginning of a Foster Care Journey

CHAPTER THREE

   Breaking the Silence: Cathy's First Book

CHAPTER FOUR

   Stories of Healing and Transformation

CHAPTER FIVE

   The Writing Process: Turning Pain into Purpose

CONCLUSION

INTRODUCTION

Cathy Glass is not just an author; she is a voice for the voiceless, a beacon of hope for children lost in the darkest corners of life. Her name has become synonymous with fostering, resilience, and the transformative power of love. But beyond the books, the accolades, and the media attention lies a woman whose journey is marked by compassion, dedication, and an unwavering commitment to healing broken lives.

Cathy was born into a world that, by her own account, was ordinary and unremarkable. She grew up in a modest home where love was abundant, but luxuries were few. Her early life was shaped by the values instilled in her by her parents—values of empathy, kindness, and the importance of family. It was these very values that would later guide her through the most challenging moments of her fostering career.

As a child, Cathy was naturally drawn to stories. She devoured books, losing herself in the pages of fiction and non-fiction alike. The characters she encountered in her readings became her companions, teaching her about the vastness of human experience. It was through these stories that Cathy first learned about the harsh realities faced by some children—realities that were far removed from her own. This early exposure to the suffering of others planted the seeds of compassion in her heart, seeds that would grow and flourish in the years to come.

Cathy's journey into fostering began not with a grand plan, but with a simple realization. She had always known that she wanted to make a difference in the lives of others, but it wasn't until she became a mother herself that she truly understood the depth of that desire. The love she felt for her own children was overwhelming, and it opened her eyes to the plight of those who were not as fortunate. She began to see the world through the eyes of the vulnerable, the abused, and the neglected. It was a perspective that would change her life forever.

The decision to become a foster carer was not an easy one. Cathy knew that it would be challenging, that it would test her in ways she could not yet imagine. But she also knew that it was something she had to do. The thought of children suffering in silence, with no one to protect them, was unbearable to her. She felt a deep sense of responsibility, a calling that she could not ignore. And so, with the support of her family, Cathy embarked on the path that would define her life's work.

Cathy's first placement was a young boy named Michael. He was small for his age, with eyes that spoke of a pain far beyond his years. Michael had been through more in his short life than most people could imagine, and it showed. He was withdrawn, fearful, and deeply mistrustful of adults. Cathy knew from the moment she met him that this would not be an easy case, but she also knew that she could not give up on him.

The early days were difficult. Michael would not speak, would not engage, and often lashed out in anger.

Cathy spent countless hours trying to break through the walls he had built around himself, offering him love and patience in equal measure. It was a slow process, but eventually, Michael began to open up. He started to trust her, to see her not as another adult who would hurt him, but as someone who genuinely cared. It was a breakthrough, and it marked the beginning of a journey that would change both of their lives.

Cathy learned a lot from Michael—about trauma, about resilience, and about the incredible capacity of the human spirit to heal. But perhaps the most important lesson she learned was about the power of love. Michael taught her that love is not always easy, that it often requires great sacrifice and patience, but that it is ultimately the most powerful force in the world. It was a lesson that would guide her through the many challenges that lay ahead.

Cathy had always been a storyteller, but it wasn't until years into her fostering career that she decided to share her experiences with the world. The idea came to her after a particularly difficult case, one that left her questioning everything she thought she knew about fostering. She realized that there were stories that needed to be told, stories that could shed light on the often-hidden world of foster care. She began to write, not with the intention of becoming an author, but simply to make sense of her own experiences.

Her first book, "Damaged," was a raw and unflinching account of her time with a young girl named Jodie. Jodie had been through unimaginable trauma, and her behavior reflected the pain she carried inside. Writing about Jodie was not easy for Cathy. It forced her to relive the most difficult moments of their time together, to confront the emotions she had tried so hard to keep at bay. But it was also cathartic. By putting her experiences down on paper, Cathy was able to process her own feelings and gain a deeper understanding of what she had been through.

"Damaged" was an instant success. Readers were drawn to Cathy's honest and compassionate storytelling, and the book quickly became a bestseller. But more importantly, it brought attention to the issues faced by children in care. It opened people's eyes to the realities of fostering, the challenges faced by both the children and the carers, and the profound impact that love and support can have on a child's life. The success of "Damaged" was a turning point for Cathy. It gave her a platform to share her experiences and to advocate for the children who had been entrusted to her care.

Over the years, Cathy has written numerous books, each one a testament to her commitment to fostering and her deep empathy for the children she cares for. Her books cover a wide range of topics, from the heartbreaking stories of abuse and neglect to the uplifting tales of resilience and recovery. But no matter the subject, each book is infused with Cathy's warmth, compassion, and unwavering belief in the power of love to heal even the most broken of lives.

Cathy's writing is more than just a chronicle of her experiences; it is a form of therapy, both for her and for her readers. For Cathy, writing is a way to process the emotions that come with fostering, to make sense of the often-painful realities she encounters. It is also a way to honor the children she has cared for, to give them a voice, and to share their stories with the world. For her readers, Cathy's books offer hope and inspiration. They show that no matter how difficult life may be, there is always the possibility of healing, of finding a way forward.

But perhaps most importantly, Cathy's books have brought attention to the need for more foster carers. Through her writing, she has shown that while fostering is not easy, it is also one of the most rewarding things a person can do. She has inspired countless people to consider fostering, to open their homes and their hearts to children in need. And in doing so, she has changed the lives of not only the children she has cared for but also the countless others who have been touched by her words.

CHAPTER ONE

Early Life and Background

Cathy Glass was born and reared in a modest and close-knit family. Her parents, while not wealthy, were committed to providing their children with a secure and caring environment. Her father was a dedicated guy who worked a steady job to support the family, while her mother was a housewife who taught strong qualities of love, compassion, and resilience in Cathy from an early age.

Cathy grew up in a family with deep relationships from birth. Her parents believed in the necessity of assisting others, which became a guiding theme in Cathy's life. Her mother played a significant role in creating Cathy's caring attitude. She would frequently accompany Cathy to see neighbors or family friends who were ill or in need of assistance, teaching her the value of community and empathy.

Cathy grew up with siblings who became her frequent companions and confidants. The Glass siblings' relationships were typical of the time, with occasional conflict but also great affection and loyalty. The complexities of her family taught Cathy the value of patience, understanding, and communication—qualities that she would later need in her fostering adventure.

Cathy's upbringing was marked by the loss of a close family member, which had a significant impact on her. This early experience with sadness made her realize the fragility of life and the value of emotional support. Cathy first saw the power of compassion and care in assisting someone in healing from emotional suffering at this trying time. This incident influenced her approach to fostering, as she was frequently the one assisting youngsters in dealing with their own traumas.

Cathy was an inquisitive child with a natural desire to learn. She excelled at school, especially in topics requiring a grasp of human nature and society, such as literature and history. Her teachers recognized her empathic character and frequently encouraged her to participate in activities that involved helping others, such as peer mentorship and charity event planning.

Cathy was lucky to have teachers who noticed and encouraged her abilities throughout her school years. Mrs. Thompson, Cathy's English teacher, saw her talent for storytelling and encouraged her to write. Mrs. Thompson's encouragement influenced Cathy's later decision to become an author. She assisted Cathy in honing her writing skills, allowing her to articulate her ideas and emotions more clearly, a talent that would later be crucial in chronicling her foster care experiences.

Cathy was deeply interested in her local community from a young age. She engaged in a variety of social and charity activities, including assisting at local shelters and organizing food drives. This involvement broadened her understanding of the difficulties experienced by less fortunate individuals and families, reinforcing her determination to make a difference in the lives of others.

Cathy was also inspired by the literature she read and the media she used. She was particularly drawn to stories of perseverance and kindness. Books like Harper Lee's "To Kill a Mockingbird," which dealt with themes of social justice and empathy, left an indelible influence on her. These stories contributed to her growing sense of responsibility for others and desire to protect the defenseless.

Cathy's decision to become a foster carer did not happen suddenly. It was the result of years of personal experience combined with a strong desire to help others in need. In her early twenties, Cathy began to seriously consider fostering as a means to give back to the community. The notion spoke to her inner compassion and the principles instilled in her during her upbringing.

When Cathy met a close friend who was already active in fostering, it marked a watershed moment in her path to become a foster parent. This acquaintance told anecdotes about the children she had cared for and how it had impacted their lives. These stories really impacted Cathy, and they fueled her desire to learn more about fostering. Her friend's encouragement and support were critical in Cathy's early steps toward being a foster parent.

Cathy received intensive training prior to becoming a foster carer. This training was both enlightening and demanding since it forced her to face some of the hard realities of child welfare. However, it also provided her with the necessary tools and expertise to give the best possible care for the children she would eventually foster. The training classes included a wide range of topics, including child psychology, trauma management, and the legal elements of foster care.

Cathy's first experience as a foster carer was both challenging and gratifying. She was assigned a little child who had been removed from an abusive environment. The toddler was aloof and afraid, but Cathy's patience and nurturing gradually broke through the child's defenses. This first placement proved for Cathy that fostering was her actual calling. The encounter was emotionally charged, but it also strengthened her faith in the transformational power of love and care.

The early days of fostering were not without difficulties. Cathy had to manage the complications of establishing trust with children who had been abused and misled by their caregivers. She experienced emotional tiredness, self-doubt, and the unavoidable pain of saying goodbye to children who had moved on to permanent homes. However, she faced each difficulty with resilience and a strong commitment to her position. The victories, such as seeing a youngster smile for the first time in months, made all the effort worthwhile.

Cathy was supported throughout her fostering journey by a network of family, friends, and other foster caregivers. This support system was critical in helping her deal with the emotional demands of fostering. Her family, in particular, was crucial in providing stability and security to both Cathy and the children in her care. The companionship and shared experiences with other foster carers gave Cathy a sense of community and belonging, which strengthened her commitment to fostering.

As Cathy continued to foster, she felt a stronger desire to share her experiences with a larger audience. She hoped that by sharing the tales of the children she cared for, she could raise awareness about the issues that vulnerable children confront, as well as the value of fostering. This prompted her to start writing her first novel, "Damaged," which went on to become a bestseller and touch the hearts of readers worldwide.

CHAPTER TWO

The Beginning of a Foster Care Journey

Cathy Glass' venture into the realm of foster care was not something she had planned from an early age. Like many others, her life began in a more traditional manner. She worked as a public servant, which provided her with stability and consistency. However, her life changed when she decided to leave her work to start a family. Her decision to emphasize family stemmed from a strong desire to nurture and care for others, but fate had other intentions.

Cathy and her husband had hoped to have their own child, but despite their best efforts, they were faced with the painful truth of infertility. This era was marked by intense mental turmoil and a sense of loss, as the ideal of having their own kid seemed to drift away. During this tough period, Cathy came across an advertisement in her local newspaper. The advertisement was straightforward: a young girl needed a foster home. This was a watershed event for Cathy, and she was immediately drawn to the concept of fostering.

Fostering had never been considered before, but something about the advertisement appealed to her. Perhaps it was the knowledge that there were children out there that needed as much love, care, and a safe place to live as she did. Cathy applied to be a foster carer without hesitation, motivated by a genuine concern for children and a desire to make a difference in their lives.

The procedure of becoming a foster carer was not immediate. It included rigorous testing, interviews, and training. The authorities needed to ensure that Cathy and her husband were prepared to handle the difficult emotional and practical demands of fostering. They took courses, performed house evaluations, and had in-depth discussions about their goals and talents. This was a learning experience for Cathy, who quickly understood that fostering meant more than just providing a roof over a child's head; it required understanding their trauma, being patient with their healing process, and offering consistent, unconditional care.

When Cathy was eventually approved as a foster carer, she felt both excited and concerned. The authorization was more than just a formal confirmation of her powers; it was a genuine admittance that she was about to embark on a journey that would alter her life forever. The first child she welcomed into her house was a young girl with a horrible past, a child who had witnessed more pain and instability than most people could bear. For Cathy, this was the start of a life-changing event that would expose her to the often terrible reality that vulnerable children endure.

The early days of fostering were not without difficulties. Cathy noticed immediately that these children's emotional and behavioral problems were extensive and complex. Many of the youngsters had been neglected, abused, or abandoned, and as a result, they frequently engaged in undesirable conduct. Tantrums, resistance, and bouts of withdrawal taxed Cathy's patience and determination.

One of the most difficult difficulties was the emotional toll fostering had on Cathy herself. She frequently felt emotionally weary after investing time and energy to caring for these children. The children's sadness became her own, and she questioned whether she had the strength to keep on. Fostering was a huge duty that required Cathy to develop emotional resilience over time.

Despite these challenges, there were some moments of triumph that made the voyage worthwhile. Cathy immediately recognized that tiny triumphs were the most important. The first time a child smiled honestly, expressed thanks, or even allowed themselves to be vulnerable, it reaffirmed Cathy's dedication to foster care. Every child's improvement, no matter how tiny, demonstrated the power of love, patience, and tenacity.

Cathy's ability to connect with these youngsters on an emotional level was one of her most valuable skills as a foster mom. She saw that fostering was not about healing the children or erasing their pasts, but rather about providing a safe and caring environment in which they could recover at their own time. This technique demanded a great deal of patience, as progress was sometimes slow and setbacks were frequent. Cathy remained consistent in her view that every child, no matter how wounded, deserved the opportunity to heal.

Cathy gradually developed a variety of strategies for dealing with the problems of fostering. She learned the value of self-care and realized that she needed to look after her own mental and emotional health in order to be a good parent. She also developed a support system of other foster caregivers, social workers, and others who understood her unusual circumstances. This network provided her with the necessary support and assistance to get through challenging circumstances.

One of the most important lessons Cathy learned was the value of setting boundaries. While her natural urge was to give ceaselessly, she realized that fostering required a delicate balance of giving and retaining her sense of self. She learnt to say no when necessary and to prioritize her own needs alongside those of the children she sought. This was not an easy lesson to learn, but it was critical for her future ability to nurture effectively.

Cathy's early experiences as a foster caregiver taught her significant skills that will help shape her future approach to fostering. One of the most essential lessons I've learned is that fostering isn't about perfection. Every child is different, so what works for one may not work for another. Cathy learned to be adaptable, to tailor her approach to each child's unique requirements, and to let go of the notion that she had all the answers.

Another important lesson was the value of patience. Many of the children Cathy fostered had been through tremendous trauma, and their healing process was not linear or predictable. There were moments of improvement followed by setbacks, and Cathy learned to celebrate small victories rather than becoming discouraged by the difficulties. She realized that healing took time, and the most important thing she could provide was her steady and loving presence.

Cathy also learned the importance of empathy. She learned that putting herself in the shoes of the children allowed her to better comprehend their behavior and respond in a caring yet effective manner. This empathic attitude enabled her to develop trust with the children, which was critical to their recovery. These youngsters struggled to trust, but with Cathy's persistent and gentle care, they began to open up and recover.

Through her early cases, Cathy learned the value of collaboration. Fostering is not something that can be done alone; it takes a team effort. Cathy collaborated with social workers, therapists, and other professionals to make sure the children received the care they needed. She also spoke with the children's birth relatives when needed, emphasizing the significance of maintaining these connections wherever possible.

Finally, Cathy's early experiences as a foster carer provided ample learning opportunities. She endured trials that tested her fortitude and perseverance, but she also saw the amazing benefits of assisting a youngster in recovery. These early cases paved the way for Cathy's future as a foster carer and author, instilling in her a strong sense of purpose and dedication to the children she looks for.

Cathy's foster care experience was both challenging and rewarding, but it helped shape her into the compassionate and dedicated foster caregiver she would become. Her tale demonstrates the power of love, patience, and tenacity in the face of tragedy, and it should serve as an example to anybody considering a career in foster care. Cathy's journey has not only impacted the lives of the children she has cared for, but it has also raised awareness about the significance of foster care and the tremendous effects it can have on both children and caregivers.

CHAPTER THREE

Breaking the Silence: Cathy's First Book

Before becoming well-known in the field of fostering and child welfare literature, Cathy Glass contributed significantly to health and social issues through her work. Her contributions to prominent journals such as The Guardian and the Evening Standard demonstrated her acute understanding of the socioeconomic challenges confronting the impoverished, laying the groundwork for what would later become her life aim. These early pieces, while devastating, were merely the beginning of Glass' quest to shatter the silence around the often-hidden world of fostering.

Cathy's debut novel, Damaged, was inspired by her own experiences as a foster parent. After years of caring for children abandoned by those who were supposed to protect them, Cathy felt obliged to share their tale with the world. These were the stories of children who had been silenced by abuse and neglect, and whose voices were frequently ignored in a society that didn't fully understand the gravity of their situation. Cathy realized that by writing about these children, she could not only give them a voice, but also raise awareness about the reality of foster care—a world that, despite its importance, remained shrouded in mystery.

Cathy's decision to write Damaged was more than just a literary project; it was deeply personal. Jodie, the little child at the center of this story, was one of Cathy's most demanding patients. Jodie's history was fraught with unfathomable tragedy, and her actions revealed the deep scars left by years of abuse. For Cathy, conveying Jodie's story entailed more than just documenting the daily realities of foster care. It was about revealing the emotional and psychological challenges that children like Jodie confront, which society may find too upsetting to comprehend.

Writing Damaged was both cathartic and difficult for Cathy. Her experiences were authentic and unfiltered, providing an accurate picture of life as a foster carer. However, being honest presents its own set of challenges. Cathy had to strike a delicate balance between protecting the identity of the children she cared for and providing the authenticity their experiences merited. This means that every detail in the book was methodically prepared, with pseudonyms used to mask the identities of those responsible.

Cathy found it difficult to explain her personal experiences. Revisiting Jodie's unhappy circumstances, as well as the difficulties they both faced in breaking these limits, triggered terrible memories. Cathy realized, however, that these stories needed to be spoken, not only for Jodie's sake, but for all of the children who had experienced similar tragedies.

Cathy's previous experience writing about health and social issues prepared her to approach this sensitive topic with care and respect. Her writing was not intended to sensationalize the suffering, but rather to convey an accurate depiction of the difficulties and accomplishments associated with fostering. She wanted readers to understand the intricacies of these situations and see the children as individuals with strengths and potential, not as victims.

Damaged, published by HarperCollins in 2007, was Cathy Glass' debut as a professional memoirist. The book had an instant and substantial impact. Cathy's writing drew readers in with its emotional honesty, while Jodie's tragic but hopeful story moved many people. For many readers, Damaged was more than a story; it was an awakening. It educated readers on the realities of child maltreatment and the challenges that foster carers face, bringing these often-overlooked issues to the forefront of public consciousness

The book's popularity demonstrated Cathy's ability to connect with her readers on a deep emotional level. Her portrayal of Jodie's pain, as well as the difficulties Cathy faced as her foster mother, resonated with people all around the world. Many others were inspired by Cathy's bravery in sharing her personal experiences, as well as the resilience and determination of the children she wrote about.

Prior to the release of Damaged, Cathy built a reputation as a keen and compassionate writer in her journalism career. Damaged, on the other hand, elevated her work, allowing her to reach a broader audience and make a greater effect on the conversation about child welfare. The book not only raised awareness about the difficulties of fostering, but also inspired readers to consider becoming foster carers themselves. It aimed to decrease the stigma associated with foster children by demonstrating that, with the right help, they can overcome their pasts and build better futures.

Damaged's success encouraged the publication of Cathy's numerous other fostering memoirs, each of which shed light on a different aspect of the foster care experience. Books such as Will You Love Me? (2013), which tells the story of her adoptive daughter, as well as Nobody's Son, Cruel to Be Kind, and A Long Way From Home, helped to establish Cathy's image as a key figure in child welfare. These volumes, which take place before the events of Will You Love Me?, were published later and provide readers with a more in-depth look at Cathy's experience as a foster parent and the children she has cared for.

Cathy's later works, including An Innocent Baby (2021), Neglected (2022), and A Family Torn Apart (2022), explored the complexities of fostering, stressing the different challenges that foster caregivers and children face. Each work has contributed to Cathy's reputation as a compassionate and perceptive writer dedicated to giving voice to the voiceless and raising awareness about the serious issues that affect society's most vulnerable children.

The significance of Damaged and Cathy's subsequent novels for readers and society cannot be overstated. Cathy's work has informed the public on the reality of foster care while also promoting positive change. Her efforts have inspired many others to become foster parents, assist low-income children, and advocate for improved child welfare laws and practices. In doing so, Cathy Glass has left an indelible mark on the lives of countless children and families, as well as on society at large.

CHAPTER FOUR

Stories of Healing and Transformation

Cathy Glass's experience as a foster carer has been distinguished by multiple stories of healing and change, each of which demonstrates the strength of the human spirit and the remarkable impact that love, patience, and understanding can have on a child's life. Cathy has cared for numerous children over the years, each with a distinct narrative of grief, struggle, and, eventually, hope. In her works, she tells these tales to the public, giving voice to the voiceless and shedding light on the often-hidden realm of foster care. The following are some of the most moving stories from her experience, demonstrating the transformative power of fostering.

Each child who comes into Cathy's care has a background of pain and loss. However, with Cathy, they discover not only a home, but a place where they may begin to recover. Cathy rebuilds these children's lives with care, understanding, and unshakable commitment, giving them a chance at a brighter future. The case studies below provide a peek into the lives of some of the children Cathy has cared for, highlighting the tremendous transformations they experienced throughout their time with her.

Jodie was one of the most difficult cases Cathy had ever encountered. When she first arrived at Cathy's house, she was a terribly unhappy and reclusive child. At the age of eight, Jodie had already endured more anguish and suffering than most people do in their lifetime. She had been terribly abused, both physically and mentally, and as a result, she had developed a variety of complicated behavioural problems. Jodie would lash out aggressively, yell, and refuse to communicate with anyone. She was a child in severe need of assistance, but she had lost her ability to trust others.

Cathy quickly realized that in order to assist Jodie, she needed to give her with a safe and stable atmosphere in which she could start to feel secure. But it was not simple. Jodie's trauma was so deep that it required months of gentle, loving care for her to open up. Cathy spent hours each day talking to Jodie, telling her that she was safe, and Jodie gradually came to trust her. One of the most significant breakthroughs occurred when Jodie finally mustered the courage to discuss what had happened to her. It was a terrible moment, but it also marked the beginning of the healing process.

Jodie gradually began to change. She grew less combative, more ready to interact with others, and even started smiling again. Cathy's unwavering support and encouragement gave Jodie the resolve to confront her past and start moving forward. Jodie had changed by the time she left Cathy's care; she was still delicate, but she was stronger and had a renewed sense of optimism.

Tayo's tale exemplifies how foster care can improve lives. Tayo was a little child who had been through a number of painful incidents before to living with Cathy. Tayo's mother suffered from significant mental health concerns, therefore he was ignored and raised in a chaotic and unpredictable atmosphere. When Tayo arrived at Cathy's house, he was a scared and bewildered little kid. He hesitated to trust anyone, and his anxiousness was shown in frequent outbursts and tantrums.

Cathy saw that Tayo's conduct was a result of the trauma he had endured, and she knew that the only way to help him was to offer him with the stability and consistency he so desperately required. Cathy worked hard to give Tayo a structured atmosphere where he knew what to anticipate each day and felt protected. She also spent a lot of time talking to him, listening to his anxieties, and comforting him that he was now in a safe and caring environment.

Tayo slowly came to trust Cathy. He began to talk about his experiences, and Cathy was able to help him deal through his fears and anger. One of the most pivotal milestones in Tayo's journey occurred when he began to form a close friendship with Cathy's dog. Tayo found solace in the dog, which made him feel more safe and less anxious. Tayo's behavior gradually improved. He relaxed, trusted, and began to enjoy life again. By the time Tayo left Cathy's care, he was a much happier and more confident youngster, ready to face the world with a renewed sense of trust and security.

Lucy's tale is one of the most moving and inspiring stories of transformation in Cathy's foster care career. Lucy came to Cathy's care after being removed from a household where she had been severely neglected and abused. Lucy, at five years old, was dangerously underweight, hungry, and mentally damaged. She was a quiet, withdrawn youngster who had learnt not to trust humans after they had repeatedly disappointed her in the past.

Cathy understood that reconstructing Lucy's destroyed upbringing would be a lengthy and tough process. The first challenge was to deal with Lucy's physical health. Cathy collaborated extensively with doctors and nutritionists to ensure Lucy had the care and nutrients she required to rebuild her strength. But the mental traumas were much more difficult to repair. Lucy was scared of being wounded again, and it took months of gentle and loving care before she felt safe.

One of the most effective strategies Cathy employed to assist Lucy was play therapy. Lucy was able to express herself and work through her trauma in a secure and controlled atmosphere by engaging in play. Cathy also spent a lot of time simply being present for Lucy, giving her the comfort and reassurance she needed to start trusting again. Lucy slowly began to break out of her shell. She began to converse more, interact with others, and express an interest in the world around her.

The most astonishing transformation occurred when Lucy began to grin and laugh again. It was an indication that she was starting to recover, and that she was feeling protected and loved. By the time Lucy left Cathy's care, she was a lot happier and more confident youngster, ready to embark on a new chapter.

Fostering is more than just providing a child with a home; it is also about assisting them in healing from the emotional and psychological wounds they bear. The children who come into Cathy's care have frequently undergone unthinkable tragedy, and the consequences can be significant and long-lasting. As a foster caregiver, Cathy has faced the deep emotional and psychological issues that come with caring for these fragile children.

One of the most difficult problems for Cathy is reestablishing the children's trust. Many of the children that enter her care have been let down by the people in their lives, and as a result, they are hesitant to trust anyone. This lack of trust can emerge in a variety of behaviors, including anger, defiance, withdrawal, and silence. Cathy recognizes that these behaviors are a defensive strategy, allowing the youngster to protect themselves from additional harm. Her attitude is always one of patience and understanding, enabling the kid to take the time necessary to feel comfortable and secure.

Another important problem is helping the children handle their experience. Abuse and neglect can leave deep and complicated emotional scars, and it can take months, if not years, for a kid to recover. Cathy employs a variety of therapeutic strategies, ranging from talking and play therapy to simply creating a safe and caring setting in which the kid can begin to feel secure. She also collaborates closely with therapists and other specialists to ensure that the child receives the care they require.

Fostering also had a tremendous impact on Cathy herself. Caring for traumatized children can be extremely draining, requiring a lot of courage and endurance. Cathy frequently builds strong ties with the children in her care, and saying goodbye when they leave can be quite tough. Despite the hurdles, Cathy considers fostering to be a very fulfilling experience. The delight of witnessing a child heal, grow, and flourish makes all of the challenges worthwhile.

Finally, the healing and transformation experiences shared by Cathy in her books serve as a strong reminder of the human spirit's resilience as well as the transformational power of love, care, and understanding. Each child who comes into Cathy's care has a history of grief and trauma, but with her, they can begin to heal. Cathy rebuilds these children's lives with patience, understanding, and unshakable commitment, giving them a better shot for the future. The emotional and psychological impact of fostering is significant, both for the children and for Cathy, but the benefits are immeasurable. Cathy's story demonstrates the amazing influence that one individual can make in the lives of others.

CHAPTER FIVE

The Writing Process: Turning Pain into Purpose

Cathy Glass's path as an author is as engrossing as her stories. Her capacity to transform other people's great grief into a source of healing and understanding for readers all over the world demonstrates her expertise, sensitivity, and commitment to fostering. Cathy's writing approach is strongly linked to her experiences as a foster carer, where she experienced some of the most difficult and tragic situations of child abuse and neglect. Through her works, she transforms difficult situations into narratives that not only engage readers but also shed light on the often-obscure world of foster care.

Cathy Glass' storytelling is based on genuineness and compassion. She doesn't just write about the children she fosters; she becomes involved in their lives, recognizing their worries, hopes, and problems. Her technique begins well before she puts pen to paper. It begins with actually listening to the youngsters that enter her care. She listens to their stories, not just the words people say, but the feelings that accompany those words. She examines their actions, responses to various situations, and relationships with others. This level of observation enables her to obtain a thorough awareness of each child's individual circumstances.

Cathy begins writing with the child's voice in mind. She wants to capture their experiences in an honest and respectful manner. Her purpose is not to sensationalize their grief, but rather to express it in a way that reflects the reality of their position. Cathy carefully selects her words so that the reader can experience the intensity of the child's feelings without becoming overwhelmed. Her writing is direct and unembellished, which adds to its impact. By keeping her text basic, she allows the story to take center stage.

Cathy's method also includes a lot of contemplation. She frequently reads her own notes and journals from when she was caring for the youngster. These records assist her in accurately recounting events and depicting the child's story with complete authenticity. Additionally, this introspection allows Cathy to handle her own emotions about the case. Writing becomes a therapeutic exercise for her as she deals with the pain and frustration she was experiencing at the time.

Empathy is central to Cathy Glass's writing. Her ability to see herself in the shoes of the children she fosters is what makes her stories so captivating. She writes not only from her perspective as a caregiver, but also from that of the child. This dichotomy enables her to express the emotional complexities of each scenario with amazing compassion.

Cathy's empathy extends beyond the children to their families, regardless of their situation. She realizes that the parents or guardians of these children frequently come from troubled backgrounds, and she treats their stories with the same care. This does not imply that she condones or excuses destructive behavior; rather, she strives to understand it. Her writing reflects this awareness, giving readers a detailed picture of the difficulties encountered by all those involved.

Cathy's novels frequently address the themes of trust and safety, which are important to the foster care experience. She describes the painstaking process of establishing trust with a child who has been continually disappointed by the people in their lives. This procedure demands a great deal of patience and empathy, which Cathy possesses in abundance. She portrays tiny successes, such as a youngster finally making eye contact or expressing a feeling, as enormous accomplishments, which they are in the context of these children's experiences.

Empathy also drives Cathy's connections with her readers. She is well aware that many of her readers may have been through comparable horrors or know someone who has. This understanding shapes how she conveys tough information. She writes with a soft hand, ensuring that her stories are accurate but not gratuitously explicit. Her goal is to offer hope and understanding, not to re-traumatize her audience.

One of the most difficult components of Cathy Glass' writing process is balancing the need to portray an accurate story while also protecting the anonymity of the children and families involved. Cathy is deeply devoted to ensuring that her writing does not harm the people she writes about. To accomplish this, she takes numerous procedures to anonymize the specifics of each case.

First, Cathy changes the names of everyone involved. She also changes some identifying information, such as locations, dates, and exact occurrences. This protects the genuine identities of the youngsters and their families. However, these adjustments are made with care to avoid distorting the story's spirit. Cathy is diligent about retaining the narrative's integrity, ensuring that the basic sensations and emotions are true to reality.

Another method that Cathy employs is to blend aspects from other scenarios. In some of her stories, a single character may represent a combination of multiple youngsters she has fostered. This enables her to emphasize common patterns and experiences in foster care without giving particular facts about any individual case. This strategy also allows her to create a more unified and compelling narrative while maintaining the anonymity of the people concerned.

Cathy is also aware of the possible impact her novels may have on youngsters as they grow older. She contemplates how they would feel after reading about their past, particularly if they identify themselves in the novel. This consideration prompts her to make deliberate choices regarding what to include and exclude. For example, she may decide to omit particularly painful aspects that are not necessary to the broader story.

Balancing privacy and storytelling also requires ethical considerations. Cathy is acutely aware of the power dynamics at play—she is an adult writing about vulnerable youngsters who may not completely comprehend the significance of their tale being shared with the world. This understanding drives her to always choose the child's well-being over the needs of the story. If there is a choice between telling the entire story and protecting a child's privacy, Cathy will always pick the latter.

Despite these limitations, Cathy Glass writes stories that are both intensely personal and broadly relatable. Her ability to handle the issues of privacy and narrative demonstrates her expertise and genuine concern for the youngsters she cares for. Through her work, she offers voice to individuals who are unable to speak for themselves while maintaining their dignity and privacy.

Cathy Glass's writing process is a deep act of empathy and responsibility. She treats each story with the respect it deserves, turning the grief of the children she fosters into narratives that educate, inspire, and heal.

By balancing authenticity and privacy, Cathy provides an environment in which tough tales can be told without causing additional hurt. Her work not only illuminates the realities of foster care, but also acts as a beacon of hope for all who have been traumatized. Cathy Glass' novels have actually transformed grief into purpose, leaving an indelible mark on her readers and the realm of child care.

CONCLUSION

Cathy Glass's journey as a foster carer and author is a testament to the power of love, resilience, and the unwavering commitment to making a difference in the lives of vulnerable children. Over the years, she has opened her home and heart to countless children, each with their unique stories of pain, trauma, and hope. Through her nurturing care, she has not only provided these children with the stability and safety they desperately needed but has also helped them to heal and grow, often against the odds.

The story of Cathy Glass is not just the story of one woman; it is the story of the many children whose lives she has touched. It is the story of the little girl who came into her home scared and silent, only to leave confident and talkative; it is the story of the teenage boy who had never known what it meant to be loved, finally finding a place where he belonged. These are the stories that have inspired millions around the world, and they are the stories that continue to drive Cathy in her work.

Being a foster carer is not an easy task. It requires a deep well of patience, understanding, and, above all, compassion. Cathy Glass embodies all these qualities and more. Her journey into fostering began out of a simple desire to help, but it quickly became a lifelong vocation. Over the years, she has cared for children from all walks of life, each bringing with them their own challenges and heartaches. But no matter how difficult the situation, Cathy has always approached each child with an open heart and a determination to help them heal.

One of the most remarkable aspects of Cathy's approach to fostering is her ability to see beyond the surface. She understands that the behaviors that many would consider difficult or even impossible to manage are often the result of deep-seated trauma and pain.

Instead of reacting with frustration or anger, Cathy responds with empathy and understanding, seeking to uncover the root cause of the child's distress and address it with love and care. This approach has allowed her to reach children that others have given up on, and it has led to countless success stories.

Cathy Glass's impact extends far beyond the children she has directly cared for. Through her books, she has shared her experiences and insights with a global audience, raising awareness about the challenges and rewards of fostering. Her writing is both raw and compassionate, offering readers an unfiltered look at the realities of fostering while also highlighting the profound impact that a loving and stable home can have on a child's life.

Books like "Damaged," "Cut," and "The Saddest Girl in the World" have resonated with readers around the world, not just because of the stories they tell, but because of the way Cathy tells them. She writes with a deep sense of humanity, never shying away from the harsh realities but always holding onto hope. Her books have given a voice to the voiceless and have helped to shine a light on the often-overlooked issue of child welfare.

In sharing her stories, Cathy has also provided a lifeline to other foster carers. Many have found comfort and guidance in her words, knowing that they are not alone in their struggles. Her books have become a source of inspiration and support for those who, like Cathy, have chosen to open their homes and hearts to children in need.

Cathy Glass's influence extends far beyond the pages of her books. Through her public speaking engagements and media appearances, she has become a powerful advocate for children in care. She uses her platform to raise awareness about the challenges faced by foster children and the importance of providing them with a stable and loving home. Her work has helped to change public perceptions of fostering and has inspired many to consider becoming foster carers themselves.

Cathy's impact can also be seen in the changes she has helped to bring about in the child welfare system. Her advocacy has led to increased support for foster carers and has helped to highlight the need for better resources and training. She has also worked to address the stigma that often surrounds children in care, reminding the public that these children are not defined by their pasts but by their potential.

One of the most profound aspects of Cathy Glass's work is the emotional and psychological impact it has had on the children in her care. For many of these children, Cathy's home was the first place where they felt safe, loved, and valued. This sense of security is essential for healing, and it has allowed these children to begin to process their trauma and move forward with their lives.

Cathy's ability to connect with these children on a deep level is one of her greatest strengths. She listens to them, understands their fears and anxieties, and helps them to navigate their complex emotions. This connection is not just about providing physical care; it is about providing emotional support and helping these children to rebuild their sense of self-worth.

For many of the children in Cathy's care, the impact of her love and support has been life-changing. They have gone on to lead happy and fulfilling lives, carrying with them the lessons and values they learned while in her care. Cathy's influence can be seen in their success and in the way they have overcome the challenges of their past.

Cathy Glass's journey has not been without its challenges. Fostering is a demanding and often emotionally draining role, and Cathy has faced her fair share of difficult situations. From dealing with children with severe behavioral issues to navigating the complexities of the child welfare system, Cathy has had to overcome many obstacles.

But despite these challenges, Cathy has never wavered in her commitment to the children in her care. She has faced each obstacle with determination and resilience, always keeping the best interests of the child at heart. Her ability to persevere in the face of adversity is a testament to her strength of character and her unwavering belief in the importance of her work.

Cathy's triumphs are not just measured in the success of the children she has cared for, but also in the impact she has had on the wider community. Through her work, she has helped to change the lives of countless children and has inspired others to do the same. Her legacy is one of love, compassion, and the belief that every child deserves a chance to thrive.

As Cathy Glass looks to the future, it is clear that her work is far from over. While she has already made a profound impact on the lives of many, there are still countless children in need of the love and care that Cathy provides. She remains committed to her role as a foster carer, and she continues to share her experiences and insights through her writing.

Cathy's future work will undoubtedly continue to inspire and impact those around her. Her dedication to fostering and her passion for helping children heal will remain at the core of everything she does. And as she continues to open her home and heart to those in need, she will undoubtedly continue to change lives for the better.

Cathy Glass's story is one of hope and resilience. It is a reminder that, no matter how difficult the circumstances, there is always the potential for healing and growth. Her work has shown that love and compassion can overcome even the most challenging of circumstances and that, with the right support, every child has the potential to thrive.

As we reflect on Cathy Glass's life and work, we are reminded of the importance of fostering and the impact that it can have on the lives of vulnerable children. Cathy's story is a powerful testament to the difference that one person can make, and it is a call to action for all of us to consider how we can contribute to the well-being of those in need.

Cathy Glass has dedicated her life to healing broken lives, and her legacy will continue to inspire and impact future generations. Through her work, she has shown us the true meaning of compassion and the incredible power of love. And as we look to the future, we can all draw inspiration from Cathy's example, knowing that,